Grab a Volleyball

by Frederick James
illustrated by Liz Callen

Practice Decodable 60

McGraw Hill Education

Bothell, WA • Chicago, IL • Columbus, OH • New York, NY

MHEonline.com

Send all inquiries to:
McGraw-Hill Education
8787 Orion Place
Columbus, OH 43240

ISBN: 978-0-02-145479-2
MHID: 0-02-145479-5

Printed in China

8 9 10 11 12 DSS 27 26 25 24 23

Dudley ran Valley Sports Camp.

Dudley said, "Stanley, come and take this closet key. Go grab a volleyball for me."

Stanley had on his headset, but he still heard Dudley.

Stanley grabbed the key and opened the closet lock. There were balls, hockey sticks, and bats, too.

Stanley had a problem. Had he heard Dudley?
Which ball was he going to take to Dudley?

Stanley ran back with a rugby ball.
"I said volleyball!" yelled Dudley.

Dudley said, "No more headsets at Valley Sports Camp."